D1582109

Contents

Illustrations as acknowledged on relevant pages

Be safe

You should be able to have a go at everything in your Brownie Annual, but sometimes it is a good idea to get some help. When you see this symbol, ask an adult if they can lend a hand.

Published by Girlguiding UK
17-19 Buckingham Palace Road
London SW1W 0PT
www.girlguiding.org.uk

Girlguiding UK
girls in the lead

Girlguiding UK is an operating name of The Guide Association.
Registered charity number 306016. Incorporated by Royal Charter.

Girlguiding UK Trading Service ordering code 6005
ISBN 978 0 85260 242 3

All Brownie and Guide photographs © The Guide Association.
Cover photograph by Laura Ashman. Internal photographs by
Laura Ashman, Niall Hartley, Henry Iddon, Rob Johnston.

Other photographs courtesy of Shutterstock unless otherwise stated.

Girlguiding UK would like to thank all the Brownies and their Leaders
who took part in the development and production of this resource.

Brownie Advisers: Sue Waller, Liz Bennett
Project Coordinator: Amy Douglas
Written by Alison Griffiths, Helen Mortimer, Mariano Kalfors,
Kate Durrant, Anna Smirnova, Abigail Latter, Hannah Rainford,
Claire Britcher
Project Editor: Alison Griffiths
Designers: Helen Davis, Angie Daniel, Rachel Doe, Caroline Keyzor,
Ana Salgado
Cover design: Angie Daniel
Production: Les Girling, Wendy Reynolds
Printed by Pindar Graphics

Readers are reminded that during the lifespan of this publication there
may be changes to Girlguiding UK's policy, or legal requirements, that
may affect the accuracy of information contained within these pages.

Brilliant Brownies

Being a Brownie is totally brilliant! Brownies is a special club where you can make new friends and have lots of adventures!

What do Brownies do?

Brownies have all kinds of fun, from playing games and making things to doing badges, going on trips and helping other people. If you are lucky you might even go on holiday with your Brownie friends!

The Brownie Promise

All Brownies make this special Promise. There are Brownies in countries all over the world, and they make a Promise like this too!

I promise that I will do my best:
To love my God,
To serve the Queen and my country,
To help other people
And
To keep the Brownie Guide Law.

The Brownie Guide Law is: A Brownie Guide thinks of others before herself and does a Good Turn every day.

Sixes

Each Brownie belongs to a small group called a Six. The leader of the group is called the Sixer.

When you see this 'Sixer' sign in your *Brownie Annual*, you will find ideas for things you could do with your Six. Why not ask your Brownie Leader if you can try them?

Brownie badges

There are lots and lots of badges that Brownies can choose to do. Whatever you like doing, from cooking and crafts to music or sports, there will be a badge for you!

You can find out about all the badges in the *Brownie Badge Book*. If you have not got a *Badge Book*, ask your Leader if you can look at hers.

On most pages in your *Brownie Annual*, you will see this 'Badge link' sign. If you had fun doing the activity on the page, you might like to try the badge in the picture.

Artist

Badge link

Your Brownie Facts

I am a Brownie in the ____Shoy at the gug____ Pack.

I am in the _____ Six.

My best Brownie friends are _____ .

The best thing about Brownies is _____ .

'At Brownies I get to play with people I don't usually play with.'

Amy, 7

7

Heart to

A pretty way to show off pictures, cards or photos!

You will need

- cardboard, for example an old cereal packet
- pen
- scissors
- drinking or art straws
- masking tape
- PVA glue and spreader
- old newspaper
- paints and brushes
- thread or thin cord, about 60cm long
- three paper clips

1 Draw a simple heart shape, about 6–7cm high, on the cardboard. Cut it out. Draw round it five times on the cardboard and cut out all the shapes.

2 Cut a piece of straw, just a little shorter than the hearts. Stick it to one heart shape with tape.

3 Stick another heart on top, so the straw is in the middle. Do the same with your other card shapes, so you have three hearts.

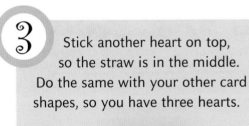

Badge link

Illustrated by Emma Metcalf

4 Mix some glue with the same amount of water. Tear pieces of newspaper and paste them all over the hearts. Make sure you leave a small hole at each end of the straws. Leave the hearts to dry.

5 Now add a second layer of newspaper scraps and leave them to dry again.

6 When they are dry, paint and decorate the hearts. You can add patterns, glitter or anything you like to make them pretty! Leave them to dry.

7 Tie a paper clip on the end of your cord, and thread the first heart on so it rests just above the paper clip. Leave a gap of about 15cm and tie on the next paper clip. Add another heart and then repeat with the last one. Now attach some cool pics to the paper clips!

Mind-benders

Test your wits against these tricky puzzles!

Puzzle 1

Which dog is exactly the same as Honey?

Puzzle 2

Follow the directions to get through the maze. The last one is missing. What is it?

North • West • North • West • North West • North • East • North • East North • East • North • West • ?

FINISH

START

Puzzle 4

How many words can you make from these letters? Can you make a nine-letter word using all the letters?

N A N O M U T I S

Puzzle 5

Find your way through the maze. Write down the letters along the path. What do they spell?

Illustrated by Gemma Hastilow

Write your answers here.

Puzzle 1		is exactly the same as Honey.
Puzzle 2	**The missing direction is**	.
Puzzle 3	**The odd one out is**	.
Puzzle 4	**The nine-letter word is**	.
Puzzle 5	**The letters spell**	.
Puzzle 6	**The hidden word is**	.

Now check page 76 to see if you were right!

10

Sandy **Ginger** **Brownie** **Biscuit** **Goldie** **Honey**

Puzzle 3

Unscramble these creatures.
Which is the odd one out?

DRAZIL

COILERCOD

KESAN

OSTORITE

ONGARD

OGLIRATAL

Puzzle 6

Fit these girls' names into the grid. What is the hidden word?

GRACIE
EMILIE
URSULA
LOUISE
NICOLA
JESSIE

start

finish

Can your brain take some more mind-benders? If it can, turn to page 26!

Surfin'!

Computer
Badge link

With one click of a mouse, you can enter the wonderful world of the web.

Have you seen the Brownies' very own website? There is so much to read and do – games you can play, activities, stories, competitions and ideas for doing Brownie badges. You can join in with the book club (see page 20 for more!) or use the advice page to help other Brownies with their problems. Check out **www.girlguiding.org.uk/brownies** for a whole lot of fun!

Whatever you like to do, you are sure to find a website all about it! Which websites do you love? Write your favourite sites here!

1 **www.girlguiding.org.uk/brownies**

2

3

4

5

The Brownie Web Safe Code

When you use the web, it is really important to stay safe. Brownies have a special Web Safe Code that you should always stick to when you are surfing.

Web safe

When using the World Wide Web I promise:
- To agree rules with my parents or guardians about the best way for me to use the computer and the World Wide Web.
- Not to give out my home address or phone number without permission.
- Not to give out the name or address of my school without permission.
- Not to agree to meet anyone who I contact on the web, unless my parents or guardians say it is all right and go with me.
- Not to put my photograph onto a website.
- To tell my parents, guardians, teacher or Leader if I find something on the web that worries or upsets me.

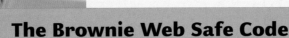

Top secret!

Every girl needs a secret diary to write her hopes and dreams in! Here are some top tips for keeping a great diary.

1 First, you need a cool diary or notebook. Find a pretty one, or decorate the cover with stickers. Don't forget to write 'TOP SECRET' on it!

2 When anything funny, exciting, scary or sad happens in your life, write it in your diary. You can write about anything you like: days out, strange dreams, arguments with your friends, plans for your future. Even the things that are too secret to tell your best friend – share them with your diary!

3 If the diary has a lock, keep the key somewhere safe. Thread it on a thin ribbon with some beads, and keep it in your jewellery box – it will look like an ordinary necklace!

4 You need a super-secret hiding place for your diary. Try one of these cunning ideas:
- Find an old hardback book with a paper cover. Slip off the cover and put it on your diary. Now you can keep it on the shelf with all your other books – and no one will know your secret!
- Keep it in a jigsaw puzzle box. Hide it under the loose pieces!
- Wrap it in an old scarf and tuck it in the bottom of a clothes drawer.

Illustrated by Cathi Mingus

STORYTIME Turn the page to read a story about one girl's worst week ever, written in her secret Diary.....

13

Gemma's Worst

When things go wrong, Gemma turns to her secret diary...

Saturday 16 May, 7pm

Met Jas, Katy and Ashvini at the park. Rode our bikes and played on the swings. Fun!! Baked beans for tea.

Sunday 17 May, 7.30pm

Rained all day. Dad took Jas and me swimming – we all jumped off the middle diving board!! Scary!! Jas stayed for tea. We had spaghetti. Can't wait for school tomorrow – Miss McCloud is giving out the parts for the play! I SOOOO want to be the cool spy. I've been wearing my lucky bracelet all week!

Monday 18 May, 5pm

A rubbish day. That lucky bracelet is going to a jumble sale. I didn't get the spy part. Even worse – Melinda got it. She thinks she is the coolest girl ever. Just because she has perfect hair and expensive trainers and a new mobile every Christmas. She was so mean to Jas last year when Jas got her glasses. And today she has not stopped posing and saying things like 'Of course, they picked someone who IS cool to play a cool spy,' and looking at me and laughing. I just ignored her.

Jas and I are aliens in the play. We get to wear green make-up and glittery costumes. I guess it's OK, and at least I'm with my best friend! Could be worse...

Tuesday 19 May, 4.30pm

It's worse. A lot worse.

This is how it happened. We were all running in from the playground when I tripped. I banged into Melinda and knocked her right over. Her lip got cut open and there was some blood (only a bit, but she cried like her head was falling off). It was a TOTAL accident. She screamed 'Look what you did, I am going to bleed to death!' I said, 'Don't be stupid, it's just a cut lip,' and I was ABOUT to say sorry but she ran off to Miss McCloud.

Next thing, Miss calls me over and says, 'Gemma, why are you bullying Melinda? She says you have been ignoring her, and you pushed her over and called her stupid. Is this true?' I was so amazed I couldn't say a single word. Miss sighed and said, 'I know you wanted her part in the play, but bullying is not acceptable. I'm very disappointed. I will have to call your parents.'

I got home from school, and Mum and Dad sent me to my room so they can talk about me. It's SO unfair!!

8pm

Feeling better. Mum and Dad asked for my side of the story. Told them everything. Mum's going to phone school in the morning. Dad made me hot chocolate with marshmallows. Yum.

Wednesday 20 May, 4pm

Worst day EVER. It started OK – Miss made me say sorry to Melinda for knocking her over, but she said she believes it was an accident, and that the whole thing is over and we should make friends again. (Like I want to be friends with Melinda.)

Then we had football and I got picked last, even though I'm the best goal scorer! I asked Katy why she didn't choose me, and she looked really scared and said, 'I don't want a bully in my team.' I said 'I'm not a bully,' and she said 'We all know what you did to Melinda,' and then she ran away!

At lunchtime no one would play with me. (Jas is off school with a sore throat.) I sat on the bench on my own. Melinda ran up and whispered 'That's what happens to bullies'. No one else talked to me at all. They look at me like I'm about to beat them up or something. They are all stupid. I don't care.

14

Week

Jas rang – she is feeling better, so I went over. We had a great talk about everything. She said, 'Don't worry Gem, I'll be back tomorrow and we'll sort them out. I've got a plan.' Of course I asked what the plan was, but she wouldn't tell me! But she is on my side!!

Friday 22 May, 4pm
Well, all I can say is, Jas is the coolest friend ever. Her plan was the best!!

PS. That was not true. I do care, I cried when I got home. Don't want to go to school in the morning.

11.30pm
Can't get to sleep. Will anyone speak to me tomorrow?

Thursday 21 May, 7.45am
Told Mum I had a sore throat like Jas, but she's making me go to school anyway. She thinks that everything is all right now. I couldn't tell her it's still all wrong. I have never, ever been so scared of going to school.

4pm
When I walked in this morning, everyone tried to get really far away from me. Someone whispered 'Bully' behind my back. Hmm, I wonder who that was... No one would be my partner in Art, so I got put with Danny Reeves, and he nearly cried. I said 'What's up?' and he squeaked like a mouse, 'Please don't bully me, Gemma!' I sort of lost my temper and shouted 'I AM NOT A BULLY!!' Guess what happened next: I got in trouble for shouting at Danny and making him cry, and now everyone in the whole world thinks I am really mean. It's the most UNFAIR thing ever and I just don't know what to do about it.

All through Maths she kept whispering to me, even when Miss McCloud told her off. Finally Miss said what she always says: 'Jasmine, your conversation is obviously much more interesting than Maths, so please share it with the rest of us.' Jas jumped right up and said, 'Oh I'm sorry Miss, I'm just trying to cheer up Gemma. She's so upset that no one is talking to her because they think she is a bully.' I was really shocked but quickly managed to pull a super-sad face. The rest of the class were staring with their mouths open. Miss said, 'Nonsense, why would anyone think that?' and Ashvini put her hand up and said, 'Melinda told us how Gemma pushed her over!'

Miss looked at Melinda and said, 'But I thought we agreed that was an accident?' Melinda went BRIGHT red and mumbled something. Miss frowned and said, 'This all sounds very silly. I would like to make it clear that Gemma is not a bully, and that no bullying will be allowed in this class. Do you all understand?' We all muttered 'Yes Miss,' and I whispered, 'Thanks Jas!'.

7pm
Jas, Ashvini, Katy and I went out on our bikes. It was cool. Jas came back for tea. We had jacket potatoes.

It's been the worst week ever, but I think everything is back to normal now. Saturday tomorrow!!

Fresh fruit

These fruity recipes will get your taste buds tingling!

Raspberry fool

This light dessert is an old-fashioned summer favourite.

Ingredients
- 300g raspberries
- 60g icing sugar
- 300g crème fraîche
- 2 egg whites

You will need
- blender, or sieve and wooden spoon
- large bowl
- small bowl
- electric or hand whisk
- metal spoon
- serving dishes

1 Whizz your raspberries in the blender till they are smooth. If you have not got a blender, squish them through a sieve with a wooden spoon.

Banana choc-ice bites

Frozen banana tastes just like ice cream – and it is even better with some chocolate!

Ingredients
- 60g chocolate
- a banana

You will need
- heatproof bowl
- saucepan
- knife
- chopping board
- cocktail sticks
- kitchen foil
- plastic tray or tub

1 Break the chocolate into pieces and put them in the heatproof bowl. Put a little water in the saucepan and place the bowl on top. The bottom of the bowl must not touch the water. Gently heat the water until the chocolate in the bowl melts. Then turn off the heat and carefully move the bowl onto a heatproof surface.

Be s

2 Put the raspberries in a large bowl. Stir in the icing sugar. Mix in the crème fraîche and stir till the mixture is smooth.

Badge link

Cook
Cook

3 Put the egg whites in a small bowl. Get a grown-up to help you whisk them till they stand up in stiff peaks. If you are using a hand whisk, this is quite hard work – but it will give you strong arms!

Be safe

4 Tip the egg whites into the raspberry mixture. With a metal spoon, gently fold them in until they are completely mixed in. Do not stir hard, or your fool will be very runny!

5 Spoon the fool into small dishes. Chill them in the fridge for an hour before eating.

2 Peel your banana and chop it into slices. Stick a cocktail stick into each slice. Spread a piece of kitchen foil over a plastic tray or tub.

Be safe

3 Dip the banana slices into the melted chocolate and put them on the foil. When you have dipped them all, pop the tray of banana bites into the freezer for half an hour. Then tuck in!

Know your fruits!

Match these exotic fruits to the pictures. If you think they look tasty, why not try some?

1
2
3
4
5
6

- Watermelon
- Passion fruit
- Lychee
- Kiwi fruit
- Mango
- Pomegranate

The answers are on page 76!

17

Snow Leopard

FACT

Next time you go walking in the forest and hear a sound like someone sawing wood, it might be a **leopard**! That's what a leopard's call sounds like. But don't worry too much. Leopards live only in Africa, Central Asia, India and China and they don't usually eat human beings. The ordinary leopard has golden fur, while the beautiful **snow leopard**, which lives high in the mountains, has a pale coat.

The **lion** is the only cat that lives in a large group, called a pride. A lioness leads the pride, and females do most of the hunting. Lions roar to let other lions know where they are. A roar can be heard from five or six miles away!

Tigers
are the world's biggest cats. The Siberian tiger weighs the same as 100 pet moggies! Every single tiger has a different stripe pattern, just like all people have different fingerprints. Not all cats hate water; tigers love to swim in lakes and ponds.

Cool cats

Unlike other big cats, **cougars** can't roar. However, they can growl, hiss, whistle like a bird and purr like a pet cat. The cougar, which lives in North and South America, is a great jumper and can leap from the ground into a tree over five metres tall.

The name 'lynx' comes from the Greek word 'to shine', and this cat has bright shining eyes. Many lynxes live in snowy places like Canada, Alaska and Russia. Their big, wide-spreading feet act like snow-shoes, supporting the cat's weight in the snow.

The **cheetah** is the fastest animal on land and can run at 70 miles an hour! The cheetah's body is built for speed. For example, its paws have hard pads, like tyres, to help it turn around when running quickly.

19

Book club

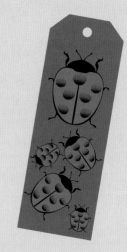

Have you heard about the Brownie Book Club?

It's a great club that anyone can join – you just have to love reading!

You can find the book club on the Brownies website, at **www.girlguiding.org.uk/brownies/bookclub**. Every month a new book is chosen. When you have read the book, you can log on and write your opinions. You can also give the book a score out of five.

All comments get posted on the website, so you can read what other Brownies thought of the book, and they can read what you said about it!

A book club is a good way of trying new books that you would not normally pick up. You might discover a new favourite book or author!

The best books ever

I love _____ by _____

because _____.

I love _____ by _____

because _____.

I love _____ by _____

because _____.

Join the club

Are you a bookworm?
Set up your own book club and
share the fun with your friends!

Who?

Get a group of your
friends together. It doesn't
matter if you all like different books –
arguing is half the fun!

Where?

If you all go to the
same school, can you use a
classroom at lunchtime? How about
the library? Is there a good spot in
the playground, like a bench or
under a shady tree? Or maybe you
could meet at someone's house after
school or at the weekend.

When?

It depends on how long
it will take everyone to read
the book you have chosen! Some people
are fast readers and will read books in
an afternoon, while others might take
longer. Think about the size of the book
you have chosen to read and then set a
date for the next meeting.

How?

Ask everyone to
come to the first
meeting with ideas for books
they would like to read. Talk
about all the ideas. You could all
vote on which book to read, or
you could take it in turns to
choose one. If you are short of
ideas, why not read the Brownie
Book Club book of the month?

Before the next meeting, think of some
questions that you can all talk about.
You might ask 'Who was the most interesting
character?', 'Was it a good ending?', 'How did
the book make you feel?' or 'Would you read
another book by this author?'. Then have your
meeting – and enjoy your book chat!

Top tips

● Try all sorts of books, even if you think
you won't like them – you might be surprised!
● Make sure everyone gets a chance to say what they
think at meetings.
● You don't just have to read stories – try poems, cartoon
books or non-fiction.
● If you can't think of books to read, ask your teacher or
school librarian if they will give you a list of ideas.

Booklover

Badge link

21

Twins together

Libby and Grace are twins – but they are very different!

One evening, Grace comes home from Brownies...

Brownies was great tonight! We did first aid.

Cool.

Sounds a bit dull!

What are you up to, Libby?

Just surfing.

Boring!!

On Saturday...

Amaani's here! We're off.

Where a[re] you going?

Dance club.

We're practising for our Brownie Dancer badge.

Why don't you come too?

No thanks, I'm busy.

Your sister never comes out.

She only likes books and computers. Boring!

Photography by Laura Ashman

22

23

24

25

More mind-benders

Have you solved all the puzzles on pages 10 and 11? Now try these!

Puzzle 8

All these animals want the tasty burger! Follow the trails to find out who gets it!

Puzzle 10

Join the dots to make a picture. What is it?

Write your answers here.

Puzzle 7		**would not visit the garden.**
Puzzle 8		**gets the burger.**
Puzzle 9		**is not in the grid.**
Puzzle 10	The picture is a	•
Puzzle 11	The pony is called	•

26

Now check page 77 to see if you were right!

Puzzle 7

How any birds can you find in the worm? Which bird would you probably not see in a garden?

Puzzle 9

Try to find these sweets in the grid! Which one is not in there?

Bubblegum
Candy cane
Chocolate
Cola bottle
Flump
Humbug
Jelly baby

Lollipop
Mint
Rock
Sherbet
Shoelace
Toffee
Wine gum

```
T E I N F E U C E T G L
C S E Y C L I O N U T I
I H T B A F U I B O B L
T O A A N H M M F P U L
C E L B D L U F P O B B
U L O Y Y H E B E P B H
P A C L C E F U L I L B
M C O L A B O T T L E E
P E H E N A T G B L G L
T P C J E L M P M O U F
S H E R B E T E N L M L
W I N E G U M O L B L N
```

Puzzle 11

Cross out all the letters that appear twice. Unscramble the rest to find the pony's name.

```
L E R A S
N C P O M
H L Y N C
O T H D E
A D P I R
```

If you have solved all the puzzles, turn to page 52 for an even bigger challenge...

Fun @ Guides

Have you thought about going to Guides when you are ten? Guides have a fantastic time doing exciting things – read these emails to see what they have to say!

Hey Luce!

Well, you asked how Guide camp was so I'll tell you. Here are some pics too. You can see what a brilliant time we had. I stayed in a tent with Shivani, Lily R, Millie, Isabel and Shannon (it rained a bit but who cares?!). We talked all night and we did loads of fun stuff too. I went canoeing – yes, I fell in the river! We cooked our meals ourselves (OK, with a bit of help!), ice cream every lunch time! Most people did abseiling but Millie and I were too scared so we made bracelets instead with the coolest beads. There were some French Guides there too. One girl, Emmanuelle, is going to be penpals with me! It was fab!

Love,
Darciexxxxxxxxxxxxx

Sixer tip

To find out more about Guides, look in the back of the *Brownies Adventure on* book. You will find some activities called *Brownies Go For It!* – why not try them with your Six?

28

Hi Hannah,

I've got to tell you about the amazing time I've just had! Have you heard of the BIG GIG? It's a massive concert, only for Guides. We've just got back and I'm sooooo excited. We saw loads of cool bands, and I screamed and sang and danced the whole time. All the Guides from around the country were so friendly. I can't wait till next year's GIG!

Anyway, gotta go and tell Mum all about it!

Hugs,
Sophie :o)

Hello Gran,

Just to let you know we got back from the hike OK! My feet are aching and really smelly! We did four miles in the end. The best bit was the picnic – I tried onion bhajis for the first time, yum! The view was brilliant from the top of Thomas Hill. Katie brought her dad's binoculars and we could see school and Leila's house. We even thought we could see you in your garden (maybe my vivid imagination!). I'd definitely go again. Thanks for sponsoring me, we have raised loads of money for the hospice. We're going to plant flowers there and make the garden really pretty.

See you soon,
Love Rebecca xxxx

Dear Amelia,

I heard you are coming to Guides soon!! Don't worry if you won't know many people. Our Guides are all really friendly and the Leaders are nice. We have a good time doing loads of stuff. Sometimes we meet outside and do sports on the playing field. We go on trips too. Last term we all went ice skating. Next summer we're going to the seaside for the day. When we meet at the hall we do games, singing, dancing, making things and stuff like that. This week we are making recycled outfits and having a fashion show!! Anyway, that gives you an idea. What do you think?

Maddy

Hi Megan,

How are you? I miss you since you left Brownies! I can't wait to go up to Guides. Your evening cooking outside must have been such a laugh. I'd have burned everything! I liked the sound of those chocolate cookies you made. Didn't you save me one? Charlie at school says she's done loads of exciting stuff at her Guides. Last week they had a dance teacher in and they all learned to salsa! She said their Leader got redder and redder and all the girls were laughing so hard at how bad she was at it! I can't wait to be ten – still two months to go!!

Bye for now!
Amerit ;)

Happy birthdays!

Use this special calendar to remember all your friends' and family's birthdays! Write the birthday date in the circle and the person's name next to it.

January

○ _____

○ _____

○ _____

February

○ _____

○ _____

○ _____

March

○ _____

○ _____

○ _____

April

○ _____

○ _____

○ _____

May

○ _____

○ _____

June

○ _____

○ _____

○ _____

July

○ _____

○ _____

○ _____

August

_____

_____

_____

September

○ _____

○ _____

○ _____

October

○ _____

○ _____

○ _____

November

○ _____

○ _____

○ _____

December

○ _____

○ _____

○ _____

Turn the page for
some fab birthday
present and card
ideas!

31

Razzle dazzle card

Add some sparkle to your friend's birthday with this super-simple, glittery card!

Craft
GLUE
Badge link

You will need

- newspaper
- piece of coloured card, folded in half
- double-sided tape
- scissors
- pens
- sequins or small stickers
- glitter
- PVA glue

1 Spread some newspaper on your table. Cut a piece of sticky tape a little bit longer than the long side of your card. Stick it onto the card, near the top. Stick another piece near the bottom edge. Trim off the ends neatly. Do not peel off the backing yet!

2 Write your birthday message in the space in the middle of the card. Use bright colours or glitter pens.

3 Peel the backing strips off the sticky tape. Arrange sequins or stickers along the sticky strips. Press them down firmly.

4 Sprinkle glitter all over the card and shake it off onto the newspaper. Glitter will stick to the tape and make it look like sparkly ribbon!

5 Finish off by sticking a few more stickers or sequins in the middle, to fill any gaps.

Alpha-biscuits

For an unusual birthday present, why not bake someone's name in tasty biscuits?

1 Sift the flour into a bowl. Add the butter or margarine and rub it in with your fingertips. Stir in the sugar.

INGREDIENTS
- 200g self-raising flour
- 60g butter or margarine
- 100g caster sugar
- 1 egg
- ½ tablespoons milk
- ½ teaspoon vanilla
- 3 tablespoons icing sugar
- 1 teaspoon cocoa powder
- cake decorations

YOU WILL NEED
bowl • sieve • spoon • mug • fork
• 2 greased baking trays • oven glove
• spatula • wire cooling tray
• small bowl • knife

2 Crack the egg into a mug. Beat it with a fork till it is mixed up. Add it to the flour mix. Add the milk and vanilla. Mix to a dough, and knead it with your hands until it is smooth.

3 Pull off a piece of dough the size of a ping-pong ball. Roll it in your hands to make a long thin sausage. Bend it into a letter shape and place on the baking tray. Now make lots more letters. If you need to join the dough strips to make a letter, pinch the join together firmly.

4 Bake at 180°C/ 350°F/gas mark 4 for 10–15 minutes, until the biscuits are golden brown. Carefully move them onto a wire tray with the spatula, and leave to cool.

Be safe

Badge link
Cook
Cook

5 Mix the icing sugar and cocoa with a little water to make a smooth icing. Spread it onto the cool biscuits and decorate!

Illustrated by Cathi Mingus

33

Dot gets sporty

'Hi, I'm Dot Com and I'm a Brownie. Last month our Pack had a new challenge...'

One evening, in our Pow-wow, Neelam had a bright idea.
'My friend Rosie's Brownie Pack are going in a Brownie football for tournament next month. Could we go in it too?' she said.

A couple of Brownies cheered but most of us groaned, and Phoebe muttered: 'Oh no, not football. I **hate** football.' I felt a bit mean, but none of us had ever really played football. How could we get a team together in just a few weeks? Sue, our Brownie Leader, had some answers...
'I heard about this too,' she said. 'The community coaches at our local football club are happy to come along and teach you all some football skills. You could learn the rules of the game and how to keep fit and healthy too.'

Genie didn't look at all happy. 'I really don't think I'll be any good at football. Can't I be the cheerleader?' she asked.

'I'm sure we can find something for everyone to do. How about it?' asked Sue. She was excited, and it would be something different – so we all voted to give football a try...

The following week everyone arrived ready for the first training session.

Neelam had borrowed her cousin's football boots and Isabelle was wearing her brother's Manchester United kit, which was about three sizes too big!

Sue introduced the football coaches, Marc and Nikki. They had brought along a huge net full of balls, some coloured bibs and what looked like traffic cones.

'First we're going to play a game called "Pirates",' said Nikki, 'so find a space and listen up.'

Nikki explained how to play the game, which she said would help with some basic football skills.

'When I shout "scrub the decks" you have to roll the ball back and forwards under your foot. If I yell "hoist the sail", throw the ball in the air and catch it,' she explained.

The game was BRILLIANT fun! If Nikki or Marc shouted 'shark attack' we all had to rush to the safety of the shark cage. Anyone who didn't make it in time got tagged and had to be a shark.

At the end of the evening Marc showed us how to cool down with a few stretches. 'Next week we'll learn the rules and start playing for real,' he said.

Phoebe was first to arrive at Brownies the following week. She was wearing a brand new pair of football trainers. 'I've been practising all week in the garden,' she said. 'My big brother showed me how to dribble the ball properly. He's really good at football.'

She wasn't the only one to have got advice at home. After his Sunday league match, Dad had dragged me to the park for a kick-around. I wanted to play in goal so he spent two hours shooting the ball at me from all angles, so I could practise catching and diving. I got covered in mud!

Marc and Nikki talked us through the rules of football and we tried playing a short seven-a-side match. Phoebe was super-fast and scored the first goal. 'You'll make a great winger,' said Nikki. Phoebe beamed and punched the air!

Everything was going well, but Genie and a few others still didn't want to play in the team. Ella had hurt her foot (her pony trod on it!) so she couldn't join in the training.

'Right,' said Marc, 'let's think what you girls can do. Ella, are you any good at taking photos? We'll need someone to get action shots of the tournament. And Genie, I've heard you want to be a cheerleader. Why don't you and the other girls put a routine together? We'll need all the support we can get.'

Everyone was excited as the tournament approached. Marc and Nikki invited us along to watch a youth team match at their club so we could see a real game. I had watched some of Dad's matches but this was really exciting - less puffing and panting and a lot more action!

The week before the tournament we had a friendly game against the Cubs who meet in our hall.

Genie's cheerleaders yelled and waved their pom-poms, and Ella took loads of photos, but we still lost 3-1. 'Never mind,' said Nikki, 'it's all good practice.'

We had to travel to the tournament on a coach. Marc and Nikki came with us and lent us an old kit, which was red with white stripes. It was a bit big but nobody minded. Genie's cheerleaders sang their songs all the way. 'Two, four, six, eight, who do we appreciate? The Red Robins!' (That was our team name.)

When we arrived, we changed into our kit and started to warm up with a few stretches and a bit of jogging on the spot. We sailed through our first game - Phoebe scored twice - but the second game ended in a 0-0 draw.

'If you win the next one you're through to the semi-final,' said Marc. It was a tough match. The other girls were bigger than us and really knew what they were doing.

'Nutmeg her!' they shouted, or 'Take it round the back!'. I didn't have a clue what they meant! In the end we lost 2-0 but everyone agreed we'd had a fantastic time.

Then - surprise! - we were awarded the trophy for the most sporting team. Sue said it was because we all worked together and didn't fight or moan at each other when things weren't going well.

In the end, winning didn't seem to matter - the best thing about the whole day was being in a team and having fun together.

On the coach back home everyone was tired. Marc said we'd done really well to learn everything in such a short space of time. And Phoebe said: 'Football's great isn't it? I think I might join a team!'

35

Friends forever

This funky bangle is a modern twist on the classic friendship bracelet! You and your best friend can make one each and swap them

You will need

- embroidery thread or thin wool, in different colours
- ruler
- scissors
- two plain plastic bangles
- sticky tape
- needle

1 With your BFF, choose some colours of thread that you both like. Now give each colour a meaning that has something to do with your friendship. For example, pink could mean 'we keep each other's secrets', blue might be 'we both love singing', or purple could stand for 'giggles'!

2 Now you are ready to make bangles with your colours. You each need to cut a piece of thread about 50cm long. Tie one end to your bangle. Stick down the short end with a tiny piece of sticky tape.

3 Wind the thread round the bangle. Keep it tight and neat, so none of the plastic bangle shows through.

Illustrated by Stuart Lynch

My fab friends

Draw some pictures of your friends here. Fill in their names, and why you like them!

Best Friends

Name rosie

I like my friend because the care about me..

Name Jemma

I like my friend because the are happy at the same ti

36

4 When you have about 10cm of thread left, cut a piece of your next colour. Tie the two ends together. Keep winding the thread. When you get to the knot, carefully stick the two short ends down with a tiny piece of sticky tape.

5 Keep winding, covering the sticky tape. Keep going in the same way, changing colours, till you have covered the whole bangle. Use longer and shorter pieces of thread to make thick or thin stripes of colour.

6 When you get to the end, loop your thread around the bangle. Pass the end of the thread twice through the loop.

7 Thread the end onto a needle and sew it back under some of the wound thread. Trim off the end neatly.

Sixer tip
You could make these bangles with your Six and all swap them!

Craft GLUE
Badge link

⭐ ⭐ ⭐ ⭐ ⭐
Star!

Name _Jamie_
I like my friend because _she helps me._

Name _adam_
I like my friend because _he is good at telling me what_

Name _Leonie_
I like my friend because _she plas with_

Your kind of music

First, get the band together and agree what sort of music you all like. Do you love fun pop songs that have you jumping up and down? Perhaps you all prefer rock and electric guitars? Maybe classical music is more your style. Or are you country-singing girls with spurs on your boots?

Girl band

Ever thought of forming a band with your friends? Here's how to make a start.

In style

You need to look as if you belong together as a group. Have a look through your wardrobes and see if you have anything that matches.

- Can you all wear the same colour clothes?
- Could you all stick to one style? How about a bright T-shirt and a skirt with some boots?
- Matching accessories will make you look like a band. Try sunglasses, cute hats or sparkly belts!
- Can you all do your hair the same way?

Turn the page to have a go at designing a star outfit!

What's in a name?

Think about what you will call yourselves. Some bands have really weird names like 'Pickettywitch', 'The Cake Sale' (yum!) or 'Vitamin C'! You could use a word you all like the sound of, like 'Pumpernickel'. You could choose someone's surname and use that, like 'The Browns'. Or maybe you want a name that says something about you, like 'The Pink Girls' or 'Sister Smile'.

Illustrated by Cathi Mingus

Dancing queens

Of course you need to dance. This is half the fun! You could just sway together, but how about making up a dance routine?

- Watch some dancers on TV and copy any moves you really like.
- Is your song fast or slow, happy or sad? What do the words say? Choose dance moves that fit the song!
- Save your best moves for the chorus. You will do this a few times so you want it to impress your audience.
- Can you sing and dance at the same time? If your dance is too lively for singing, your lead singer could just do the arm moves while the rest of you do the whole dance.
- Remember to smile!

A song to sing

What will you sing? Any good at making up songs? If not, choose your favourites and do cover versions! You can get the words to songs on the Internet if you search for the song title. If you have a karaoke machine, switch it on and get practising!

Web safe

Tune up

Here are some singing tips to make you all sound like stars:

- Never sing if it hurts to swallow. You could really hurt your voice.
- Never hold your breath when singing.
- Keep your shoulders loose and down.
- Think about the meaning of the words and try to put lots of feeling in your voice.
- Don't sing too high or too low for your voice.
- Practise in front of the mirror.
- Open your mouth wide.
- Have fun!

Show time!

Don't keep your band hidden away in a bedroom. Put on a show for your families or friends, or at Brownies! Make sure the music is loud enough, you have practised lots and you all look your sparkly best! Good luck!

Badge link

If you were in a top girl group, what would you wear on stage? Would it be head-to-toe glitter, grungy jeans or cool dance gear? Design yourself a perfect pop star outfit!

Fashion Fun!

Good designers always try to create clothes that are trendy but practical. Here are some things to think about:

- Will you be able to dance in your groovy outfit?
- It gets hot under all those spotlights – can you stay cool?
- Make sure the audience can see you – bold colours and shapes are good.

Now get creative and start designing!

Illustrated by Cathi Mingus

Brownie shopping

Brownies can buy lots of special gifts – here are just a few of them!

Cuddly teddy clip

Clip this cute fluffy bear to your bag and take him everywhere!

Order code 2602

£2.60

Mug

A colourful mug for your favourite drinks!

Order code 2388

£2.30

Towel

Bathtime is Brownie time with this bright cotton towel!

Order code 2033

£5

Cookies

Yummy all-butter chocolate chip cookies – mmm!

Order code 7012

Special offer!
For the whole of January 2009, our delicious cookies are on sale at the special price of **£2!** Usually £3.

Bracelet

This beautiful silver bracelet will make any Brownie feel special!

Order code 7413

£17.50

Fun purse
(assorted colours)

Keep your pennies safe in style!

Order code 7357

£1.75

Message to parents!

Did you know that when you buy from Girlguiding UK Trading Service all the profits go back to supporting guiding? You can see the full range of Brownie wear and products in our special parents' and families' catalogue. Order your free copy by ringing 0161 941 2237.

41

the bear who

Once upon a time, in a land called Elsewhere, there lived a young bear. Like any other bear, he lived in a cosy cave. He enjoyed the things that all bears enjoy – honey for breakfast, fish for lunch and berries for supper after a good long afternoon snooze.

One day, while fishing in the river, the young bear saw a carriage pass by. Made of gold, studded with precious stones and pulled by six white and six black horses, it was a magnificent sight. The starstruck young bear looked on in awe.

'That was the King of Elsewhere,' said an otter swimming nearby. The bear was not sure what a king was, so he asked the otter to explain.

'A king,' said the otter, 'is someone who has done a great deed. Because of that he lives in a palace, rides in a golden carriage and rules over all the creatures in the land.'

'Can anyone become a king?' asked the young bear.

'Of course,' replied the otter, 'but not the king of Elsewhere, which already has one.' The otter, though, had heard of a place called Mervyn Rutania. In that land was a fierce wild ox, the size of an elephant, which ate all the people's crops. Whoever could tame the ox would be made king.

The young bear decided he would tame the ox so that he too could become a king and ride in a beautiful carriage. But first he would finish his lunch, for he was still hungry. Being a very polite bear, he offered to share it with the otter. The grateful otter thanked him, for she was tired and hungry, and the swift fish were hard for her to catch. And so they ate together, and afterwards the bear said goodbye and set off to find Mervyn Rutania and the giant ox.

'Goodbye and good luck,' said the otter. 'I will tell all my friends that you are the kindest of bears.'

Hours later, the young bear was walking in the woods when he heard a cry for help. He looked up and saw a fox surrounded by snarling wolves. Being a brave bear, he roared loudly and chased them away.

'Thank you,' gasped the fox in relief. 'And what brings you to these dangerous woods?'

The young bear explained his quest. However, the fox shook his head and said that the ox had already been tamed. 'Fear not though,' the fox added, for he had heard of a land called Storm and a Horn of Peace. Blowing the horn would calm the stormy winds that always raged across the land. Whoever could find the horn and blow it would be made king of Storm.

The young bear decided to find the Horn of Peace instead. He thanked the fox and set off.

'Good luck,' called the fox. 'You are the best of bears and I will tell that to everyone I know.'

Illustrated by Emma Metcalf

would be king

The bear walked all afternoon, until it was time for supper. Hungry once more, he stopped for some berries. He looked around and noticed two little moles pushing and pulling hopelessly on a fallen tree. Being a helpful sort of bear, the young bear asked what was wrong.

'This tree has fallen over the entrance to our home,' said the moles sadly, 'and we cannot move it.'

The young bear heaved and pushed the tree aside, and freed the moles' home.

'Thank you!' cried the grateful moles. 'Now what brings you so far from home?' And so the young bear explained his quest once again. The moles sighed and told the bear that someone had found the Horn of Peace just a week ago. However, they told him instead of a land called Blue Hills, where there existed a magical cloak called the Cape of Good Hope. The people of Blue Hills were sad and gloomy, but whoever could find the cape and wear it would make them happy again, and would also be made king.

Can anyone become a king? asked the young bear.

The young bear thought he might as well give it a try. He thanked the moles and went on his way.

'Good luck,' cried the moles. 'You are a prince among bears and everyone shall know it.'

It was nightfall and the young bear had grown weary. Home seemed a long way away, and he missed his cosy cave. Suddenly he heard a sound from above: 'Too-whit-a-whoo.' A wise old owl swooped down and asked why a young bear was lost in the dark. So the bear explained his quest once more. The wise owl replied gravely that the Cape of Good Hope had been found long ago, and Blue Hills had a king.

'Never mind,' said the bear, for he no longer really wished to be king, and only wanted to go home.

'Wise owl, will you please help me find my way home?'

'I would be glad to help,' replied the wise owl, 'for I've heard of a King of Bears walking these woods and doing many good deeds. Follow me this way, your Majesty.'

THE END

43

Wonderful wildlife

Badge link

How well do you know your wildlife?

The UK is a fantastic place for nature lovers! Wherever you go, you are bound to see some exciting wildlife. Even if you live in a city, keep your eyes open and you will spot all kinds of birds, plants and insects.

Try this fun quiz and find out how much you know about UK wildlife! When you have finished, check the answers on page 77.

1

What is the largest mammal living in the UK?
- **a.** red deer
- **b.** muntjac deer
- **c.** roe deer

2

What kind of tree do these leaves grow on?
- **a.** oak
- **b.** beech
- **c.** holly

3

Which animals start life as tadpoles?
- **a.** frogs, toads and newts
- **b.** frogs, toads and slow worms
- **c.** frogs, toads and lizards

4

What is the name of this garden bird?
- **a.** yellowhammer
- **b.** blue tit
- **c.** greenfinch

5
What do hedgehogs love to eat?
a. roses
b. slugs and worms
c. grass

6
What is the name of this butterfly?
a. red admiral
b. peacock
c. swallowtail

7
Can you name this woodland flower?
a. cornflower
b. bluebell
c. foxglove

8
Where would this gannet make its home?
a. in a forest
b. on a cliff
c. by a pond

9
What are baby rabbits called?
a. cubs
b. pups
c. kits

10
What do ladybirds feast on?
a. leaves
b. greenfly
c. daisies

Road racing

FACT

To be a top **road racer**, you need to be fast and fit and have lots of stamina (be able to keep riding for a long time). The most famous road cycling race is the Tour de France. It takes place in France every summer, lasts more than three weeks and covers over 1,800 miles! The race course is different each year, but it always includes steep mountains. Every day, the person who is winning the race gets to wear a special yellow jersey.

Cycling is fun, good for your health and great for the planet. If you really love to cycle, why not take it up as a sport? There are lots of different sports to choose from. If you want to try any of these, search for your nearest cycling club on **www.britishcycling.org.uk**.

Make sure you **stay safe** when you are out on your bike. Always wear a helmet to protect your head. Trainers or other non-slip shoes will stop your feet sliding off the pedals. Before you cycle, check your tyres and brakes. For more safety tips, take a look at the website **www.cyclesense.net**.

Web safe

On your bike

Badge link

Cyclist

AP/PA Photos

The fastest cycling sport is **track cycling**, in which cyclists ride laps around a track at speeds of up to 40 miles an hour! In 'pursuit' races, two riders start on opposite sides of the track and have to try to catch each other. In the 'keirin', riders follow a motorbike for most of the race. The motorbike leaves the track with two and a half laps to go, and the cyclists sprint as fast as they can to the finish!

Are you tough, adventurous and happy to get covered in mud? **Mountain biking** could be the sport for you. It's about riding bikes off-road over all sorts of ground (not just mountains!). Mountain bikers need to be strong and fit, and able to look after themselves and their bikes. They like a challenge and love biking in wild country!

47

Fun and games

Try these great games — you will never be bored again!

Jacks

You need a small bouncy ball and six pebbles, dice or other small objects. These are the 'jacks'.

1 Scatter the jacks on the ground in front of you.

2 Using just one hand, throw the ball up in the air, pick up one jack and catch the ball again before it bounces!

3 Put the jack to one side. Keep doing step 2 till you have picked up all the jacks. If you miss or drop a jack or the ball, you have to start again!

4 Now scatter the jacks again. This time, when you throw the ball up in the air you have to pick up two jacks before you catch it. When you have picked them all up two at a time, scatter the jacks again and pick up three in one go, then four, and so on. When you can pick up all six at once, start again using your other hand!

Down, down, down

This is one for the garden. You need at least two people.

1 Throw a ball to each other in turn until someone drops it or doesn't catch it.

2 The first time you drop it, you must go down on one knee. The next time you go down on both knees, the third time down on one elbow, and then down on both elbows.

3 If you drop it again, put your chin on the ground too. This makes it really hard to throw and catch! It's very funny when you are all on the ground trying to play!

Doodles

Start by drawing a simple shape, like a square, a triangle or a heart. Now see if you can turn the shape into an animal, a person, a plant or something else by doodling around it. You can play this with a friend: draw a shape for each other and see if you can both make them into cool pictures!

Animal magic

This is a good one for rainy days or long journeys. You can play it with one friend or a small group.

One person chooses an animal. The rest have to work out what the animal is by asking questions like 'Is it furry?', 'Can it see in the dark?', 'Does it live in this country?', 'Is it bigger than a cat?'. When they think they know what the animal is, they can ask 'Is it a ...?' The person can only answer 'yes' or 'no'. How long does it take to find out what the animal is?

Sixer tip!

Play some of these games with your Six at Brownies!

Lunchbox of

Fed up with the same old things in your packed lunch? Try some of these easy recipes and give your taste buds a treat!

Badge link

Cheesy bread

This tasty loaf makes great sandwiches with sliced cheese and crispy salad!

1 Put all the ingredients, except the extra margarine or butter, into a large bowl. Beat with a wooden spoon until everything is well mixed together.

Ingredients
- 75g margarine or soft butter (plus extra for greasing)
- 200g self-raising flour
- 1 teaspoon baking powder
- large pinch of dried herbs
- 2 eggs
- 75g strong cheese, grated
- 150ml milk

You will need
- large bowl
- wooden spoon
- loaf tin
- greaseproof paper
- oven gloves
- wire cooling tray

2 Line your loaf tin with a piece of greaseproof paper. Grease the paper with a little extra margarine or butter. Spread your mixture in the tin and smooth the top.

3 Bake the cheesy bread at 180°C/375°F/gas mark 5 for 35–40 minutes. It should have risen and be golden brown on top. Carefully take the loaf out of the oven. Leave it in the tin for 15 minutes, then put it on a wire tray to cool.

Be safe

Illustrated by Emma Metcalf

delights

Perfect pasta

Colourful pasta salad will give you lots of energy for the afternoon! This recipe makes enough for two days.

Ingredients
- 100g pasta shapes
- 1 stick of celery
- 8 cherry tomatoes
- half a pepper
- 2 tablespoons tinned sweetcorn
- 2 tablespoons salad cream, mayonnaise or natural yoghurt

You will need
- saucepan
- sieve
- chopping board
- knife
- small bowl
- spoon

1 Put the pasta shapes in a saucepan with plenty of water. Boil them for about 8–10 minutes until they are cooked. Carefully drain the pasta through a sieve and leave it to cool.

Be safe

2 Wash your celery and pepper. Carefully chop them into small pieces. Wash the tomatoes and cut them in half.

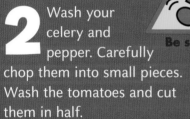
Be safe

3 Put the cool pasta, celery, pepper, tomatoes and sweetcorn into a bowl. Add the salad cream, mayonnaise or yoghurt and mix everything together. Keep your pasta salad in the fridge until you are ready to go to school!

Treasure hunt!

Your great-grandma was a famous pirate, Seven Seas Sal. In an old book of hers, you have found this secret map and some clues to lead you to the place where she buried her ill-gotten gold...

Oh no - there are some words missing from the clues! To fill the gaps, you need to solve the puzzles on pages 10-11 and 26-27. Write the puzzle answers in the gaps here: where it says 1, write the answer to Puzzle 1, and so on!

Badge link

Finding your way

Out and about

Start in the very south, where the beach is   **1** _____.

Follow the river   **2** _____ - a compass might be handy!

Watch out for   **3** _____ s   as you climb the   **4** _____ high,

Then find some   **5** _____ the colour of the sky.

Go north-west through the   **6** _____, where snakes and spiders roam,

Then creep past the   **7** _____ s - don't let them get your bones!

Heading west through swampy ground will lead you to the shore,

Now follow it to find the place where strong winds always roar.

Cross the river where you might be dinner for a   **8** _____;

Go through the desert till you see a spooky-looking   **9** _____.

Head east to find a lonely   **10** _____ upon the   **11** _____ moors.

Dig underneath it and the pirate treasure will be yours!

Now follow these directions around the island map. Put a big red 'X' where you think the treasure is! You can check your answer on page 77.

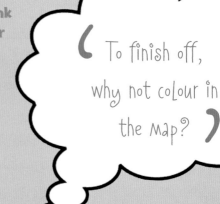

To finish off, why not colour in the map?

Illustrated by Gemma Hastilow

52

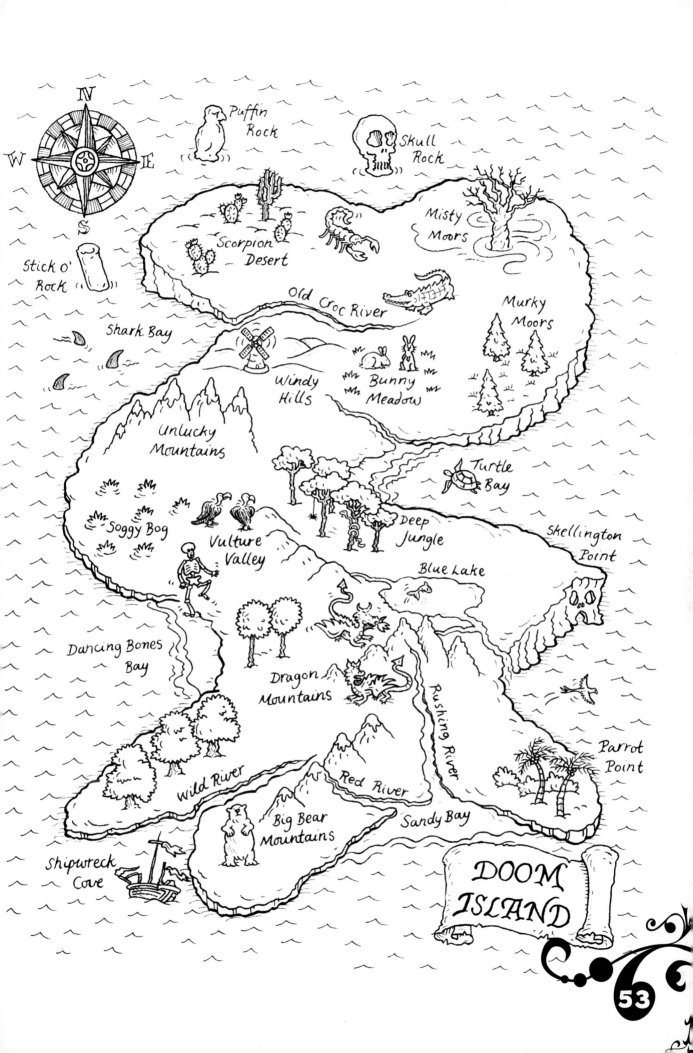

Pyjama party

Badge link

Craft
GLUE

Cook

Cook

Hostess

Everyone loves a good sleepover! Here are some ideas to help you plan the perfect night – just add your friends!

Plan ahead

Make your plans in plenty of time! Then make sure you have everything you need for the big night.

- What are you going to eat? Not just in the evening but for breakfast too. Check that your guests will like what you have chosen. There are some good food ideas on the next page!
- Where will everyone sleep? If you have a tiny bedroom, maybe the dining room or living room would be better? Make sure you all sleep in one room.
- What are you all going to do? Watch a film or play games? You could tell stories or do face painting. How about making something pretty for everyone to take home?
- Will your sleepover have a theme? Look at the next page for some great theme ideas!

Look after your friends

- Try to have an even number of people at your sleepover; four or six is best. That way no one gets left out!
- Are you going to invite a friend who only knows you? She might need some special attention to help her make friends and have a good time.
- If one of your friends gets homesick and wants her own bed, don't get cross with her! Not everyone likes sleeping away from home. If you can't persuade her to stay, ask an adult to call her parents to come and fetch her.

Illustrated by Stuart Lynch

54

A sleepover with a theme is fun and unusual! Having a theme makes it easier to plan whether there should be fancy dress, what you are going to eat and what activities and games you will have. How about:

- America – cowgirls, burgers and fries, milkshakes, movies, line dancing.
- Tropical beach party – make grass skirts from crêpe paper, mix some fruit juice cocktails, eat ice cream and dance the night away!
- Alice in Wonderland – make jam tarts (for the Queen of Hearts), have a Mad Hatter's tea party, decorate Alice bands, and wear stripy tights and enormous grins like the Cheshire Cat!
- Mexico – have a piñata (a sweetie-filled container made from card and tissue paper), hot chocolate, tortilla chips and dips, big hats and moustaches!

YOU WILL NEED

- coloured card
- felt tips
- tracing paper
- pencil
- scraps of pretty fabric or wrapping paper
- scissors
- glue
- glitter, beads or sequins (if you like)

Invitation station

Start the party in style with these funky invitations!

1 Fold a piece of card in half. On the inside, write the date of your sleepover, what time it is and where. Add the kit list so your guests know what to bring. Tell them if there is a theme or if you are dressing up.

2 Trace the pyjama shapes onto your fabric or wrapping paper. Cut them out and stick them on the front of the invitation. Jazz them up with some glitter or sequins if you want to! Now make enough invitations for all your guests!

KIT LIST

Make sure everyone brings:
- sleeping bag ● toothbrush and toothpaste ● face flannel and small towel ● pyjamas ● slippers ● clean knickers and socks ● teddy or cuddly toy.

Turn the page for some fun things to do and tasty treats to make!

55

Create some living works of art!

1 First of all, make sure no one is allergic to face paints.
If the paint itches or stings, wash it off straight away.

2 Now go to town painting each other's faces! Keep your designs simple. Try flags, butterflies, ladybirds or flowers. Do not paint near anyone's eyes.

3 Carefully wash all the paint off before laying your head on your pillow!

Spooky story

Make up a spine-tingling tale! One of you should read out the start of the story below. Then someone else takes over and makes up what happens next. Take turns to add more to the story – and see how scary you can make it!

'Last night I woke up with a strange feeling. The room was very cold and the house was silent. I got up and looked out of the window. It was dark outside but I could just see two gleaming green lights. They looked like a cat's eyes – but surely no cat could be that big? Slowly, the eyes moved closer...'

More top ideas

- Try out some cool hairstyles on each other. See page 66 for a great style!
- Put some tunes on and have a sing-along!
- Have a pyjama fashion show!

Don't forget...
- Brush your teeth before settling down!
- If you have a camera, take loads of pics of your friends having fun in their jammies!

Illustrated by Stuart Lynch

Choco-shakie!

This recipe makes two delicious chocolate milkshakes.

1 Put the milk, ice cream and drinking chocolate in the blender and whizz for about 30 seconds. Pour the shakes into two glasses.

2 Crush up the chocolate flake and sprinkle it on top of the milkshakes.

Pitta pizzazz

INGREDIENTS
- a pitta bread each
- jar of pizza topping or tomato sauce
- grated cheese
- other toppings, like chopped mushroom or pepper, sweetcorn, ham, pineapple
- dried herbs

Get the toppings ready earlier, then you and your friends can all make up your own instant pizzas. Ask an adult to help you cook them!

1 Spoon some tomato sauce over each pitta.

2 Add the cheese and any other toppings you like. Then sprinkle on a pinch of herbs.

3 Cook your pizzas under a hot grill until the cheese is melted and bubbling. Mmm!

Be safe

Moon gazing

Meet planet Earth's next-door neighbour!

Moonlight

Is the Moon made of cheese? No – it is a big ball of rock whirling through space. Although it looks like a pale Sun, it does not make any light of its own. When you see the Moon shining, you are seeing the light of the Sun bouncing off the Moon and shining back down on you.

Force of nature

Gravity is a force that pulls objects towards each other. The gravity of the Earth makes everything fall down to the ground. When you jump up in the air, gravity makes you come down again. There is no gravity in space, which is why astronauts float around!

High tide

Gravity also pulls planets and stars around. It pulls the Earth and the Moon towards each other. Earth's gravity keeps the Moon spinning around our planet in a path called an orbit. The Moon's gravity pulls the water in all the seas on Earth towards the Moon. This is why the seas have high tides and low tides.

Moon facts

- The Moon travels through space at 2,288 miles an hour!
- Even at this speed it takes 29 days to go all the way round the Earth.
- Only twelve people have ever walked on the Moon.
- No one has found any signs of aliens living on the Moon!

Illustrated by Emma Metcalf

58

Moon phases

The Moon shining in the night sky is always beautiful. But why is it sometimes round, sometimes a thin crescent and sometimes in between? Try this experiment to find out!

You will need
- ping-pong ball or polystyrene ball
- black marker pen or paint
- empty glass
- torch

1 Carefully colour or paint one half of the ball black. Leave it to dry. This is your Moon.

2 In a dark room, place the glass and torch on a table. The glass stands for the Earth. The torch is the Sun. The beam from the torch is like the Sun's rays shining on the Earth.

3 Move your Moon ball around the glass in a circle. This is like the Moon in orbit around the Earth. Make sure you always keep the white half of the Moon facing towards the Earth. You should be able to see different parts of it shining when it is at different places in the circle. Draw them in the diagram.

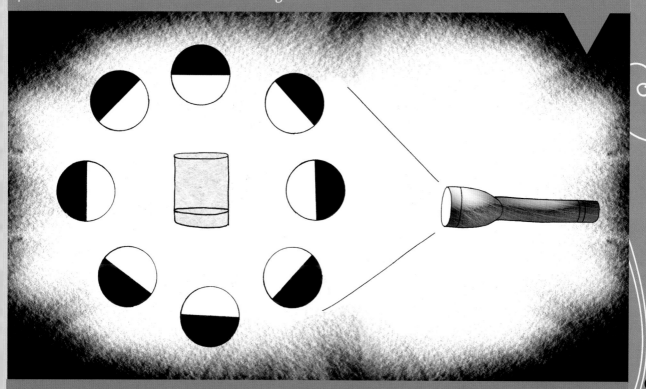

This experiment shows why we do not always see the Moon as a round shape. The different shapes are called the phases of the Moon. To try it for real, why not keep a Moon diary? Take a look at the Moon every night. Draw its shape in your diary. After 29 days, it should be the same shape as on the day you started your diary!

59

the Magical Museum

Welcome to the Magical Museum, where weird and wonderful things can happen! Travel around it at night, and choose where you go and what you do. If your story ends and you haven't visited all the rooms, try again.

Ancient Britain Room

You and your Brownie Pack, the _____ Brownies, are having a special sleepover at the museum. You have seen all sorts of things: space suits worn by astronauts, strange stuffed animals from faraway lands, and lots more.

You are sleeping in the Ancient Britain Room. Around the walls are glass cases filled with pale skeletons, rusty spears and gleaming golden jewellery.

You and your best friend _____ are far too excited to sleep. You whisper to each other until your Leader asks you to be quiet. Soon you drift off to sleep.

In the middle of the night, you wake up. Your best friend, your Leader and all the other Brownies are sleeping. You decide to explore. At the end of the room there are doors leading to four other rooms.

Where will you go first?

Explorer Room - go to A).
Space Room - go to B).
Art Room - go to C).
History Room - go to D).

A) Explorer Room

As you walk up the stairs you hear thousands of insects chirping and the sound of drumming in the distance. A giant butterfly, the size of your head, floats by. At the top of the stairs you look around. There are plants growing everywhere, and the ceiling is hidden by tall trees.

A man in green clothes and a hat is crouching down, looking up into the leaves. 'What are you looking at?' you ask.
'Shhh... don't scare it away,' he whispers. 'It's a very shy creature - the Lesser Spotted Tootingflapper. I'm going to catch it for a museum.'
Suddenly, a brightly spotted bird comes flapping noisily past. The explorer gets out a net and tries to catch it.

You remember that earlier in the day, you saw lots of stuffed animals in glass cabinets. Your Leader told you that most of the animals are now extinct. You think of telling the explorer about this.

If you tell him, go to E). If not, go to F).

Illustrated by Beccy Blake

B) Space Room

You walk into the Space Room and there is a sucking sound as the doors seal shut behind you. You're in a rocket that has landed on the Moon! Suddenly you feel very light and bouncy, because there is not much gravity.

Two astronauts are looking at a moon buggy.

'Oh no!' you hear one say.

'What's wrong?' you ask, bouncing over to them.

'Our robot is not working, and we're much too big to fit in the buggy,' one replies. 'We need to collect some moon rocks before we fly back to Earth.'

If you offer to go in the moon buggy, go to H). If you ignore them and have fun bouncing around, go to I).

H)

'I could help you – I'm small enough to fit in there,' you say. In a moment you are in the buggy, bumping along the rocky surface of the Moon. Your mission is to collect a sample of moon rock. You have to use a metal arm, which you can move with a joystick. After a few tries you manage to pick up a bit of rock. 'Mission successful!' you say into your microphone. You can hear the astronauts cheering through your headphones.

You say goodbye to the astronauts and leave through the air-sealed doors.

Where will you go next?

Art Room – go to C).
History Room – go to D).
Explorer Room – go to A).
Back to bed – go to J).

E)

'No!' you shout and the explorer misses the bird with his net.

'What is it?' he asks crossly. You explain that if people kill too many of any kind of animal, it will die out.

'Oh, I hadn't thought of it like that,' he replies, taking off his hat and scratching his head.

'You could draw them and make models later,' you suggest.

'Great idea!' says the explorer.

You go back to the stairs and the sound of insects fades away.

Now where will you go?

Space Room – go to B).
Art Room – go to C).
History Room – go to D).
Back to bed – go to G).

C) Art Room

The walls of the Art Room are covered in old paintings. They are of men in big white wigs, and women with very pale faces and beauty spots. You look closely at one of the paintings. It reaches from the floor to the ceiling and shows a beautiful girl in a purple satin dress. She is holding a small dog on her lap.

Then you realise that the girl and her dog are moving! You touch the painting and your hand goes straight through. You climb in.

The girl and her dog are being painted by a man in a funny black hat. The girl is not as beautiful as she looked in the picture. She has black teeth and smells terrible! When you saw this painting earlier, your Leader told you that it was painted in 1755. In those days people didn't have toothpaste and washed only once a month!

'You're taking far too long!' says the girl to the painter. 'Tess wants a walk.'
'I'm not taking her,' growls the painter. 'That servant girl can do it.' He points at you.

If you offer to take the dog for a walk, go to K). If you say 'No way, she's got fleas!', go to L).

K) 'Come on Tess!' you call and the dog races over to you. You both run outside. The streets are filled with people selling vegetables and pies, carrying heavy loads of firewood, drinking mugs of beer, chatting and arguing. Chickens run everywhere and one man is herding some sheep down the middle of the street! You and the dog have a good long walk. When you get back, she is tired out! You slip back out through the painting.

Where will you go next?

Explorer Room - go to A).
Space Room - go to B).
History Room - go to D).
Back to bed - go to M).

Illustrated by Beccy Blake

F) While the explorer catches the bird, you hear your best friend calling your name. She's waking you up because she feels homesick. You talk for a while and then go back to sleep. **THE END.**

I) As you play around, you notice that the engines make a noise every time you breathe out. Your Leader wakes you up and tells you that you were snoring! Turn over and go back to sleep. **THE END.**

O) You skate towards the boy. The ice becomes thinner and you too fall down a hole! But then you wake up. Your best friend has knocked over some water, which has got into your sleeping bag and made you cold and wet! **THE END.**

P) When you wake up in the morning, your legs feel really stiff! You run into the History Room and look at the Victorian display. At the back is a model of a small boy, wrapped in a blanket and drinking a big mug of hot tea! **THE END.**

G) You wake up in the morning. As you leave the museum, you notice something strange. When you arrived yesterday there were some stuffed birds in a cabinet. They have disappeared and in their place are some drawings and wooden models... **THE END.**

J) You wake up in the morning. You have time for one last look around the museum. In the Space Room you spot something that wasn't there before. Next to the big adult space suits is a small child's one! **THE END.**

L) You wake up with a really itchy leg! You rub it till it stops itching, then snuggle down and go back to sleep. **THE END.**

M) You wake up in the morning and tell your best friend all about your strange dreams. There's just time to have a final look around. In the Art Room you see the big painting of the girl. The small dog is curled up on her lap, happily asleep! **THE END.**

D) History Room

The History Room has glass display cabinets showing models in scenes of past times. You walk past one that shows people watching a Shakespeare play, and another showing a family's living room in World War Two. At the end of the room you see that one of the displays is open and snow is drifting out.

The sign above the display reads 'The Victorian Age'. You go inside. It's winter and people are ice-skating on a lake. A girl and her mother skate over. They are wearing black dresses that reach from the top of their necks to below their ankles.
'Hello,' says the girl, looking at your pyjamas. 'What strange clothes you are wearing – you must be very cold.'
'I am a bit,' you say, shivering.
'Come with us,' says the woman. 'Elsie has a spare pair of boots and a coat.'

Once you're dressed warmly, you go skating on the ice. You're very good at it, which is strange because you have only ever been ice-skating once in your life. You do spins and jumps. Elsie and her mother are very impressed. Just then, you hear people shouting on the other side of the lake – a boy has fallen down a hole in the ice! You start to skate towards him.
'Wait!' says Elsie. 'The ice is thin over there – it's dangerous. And besides, there are some grown-ups helping him.'

If you stay with Elsie and her mother, go to N). If you try to help the boy, go to O).

N) You stay with Elsie and her mother and watch the boy being rescued. After you've changed back into your pyjamas and said goodbye, you go back to the museum. Now where will you go?

Art Room – go to C).
Space Room – go to B).
Explorer Room – go to A).
Back to bed – go to P).

Cheeky!

FACT

One amazing thing about hamsters is their way of carrying food. They stuff any food they find into pouches inside their cheeks, and take it home to hide and eat later. You might think your hamster is being very greedy when it sits in the food bowl and crams its pouches full of food. However, it will store most of the food in its house and have snacks later!

Ham-tastic!

Find out how hamsters live in the wild – and how you can help them to be happy as pets!

Wild hamsters come from Syria, a hot country in Asia. They dig burrows and tunnels to live in. Living underground keeps them cool – and safe from danger! Hamsters are born diggers, so pet hamsters need plenty of wood shavings to burrow in. They also love to run through tunnels such as old toilet roll tubes!

When you live in the desert, there isn't much food around! Wild hamsters run around all night looking for enough food – they can travel as far as five miles in one night! A pet hamster will be unhappy if it can't get enough exercise. It needs a big cage with a solid wheel inside, so it can run whenever it likes. It should also be let out of the cage to play every day.

Wild hamsters eat seeds, grains and small amounts of fresh leaves. To give pet hams a healthy diet, feed them on special dry food mixes that you can buy in pet shops. They also like small treats of fresh veg, fruit, cheese or nuts – but not too much!

Hamsters do not like other hamsters much! In the wild they live alone and will fight any strange hamster who comes near their home. This is because food is hard to find, and they do not want to share it! A pet hamster should live on its own. As long as you play with it every day, it will be quite happy.

super style

Stand out from the crowd with this unusual hairstyle!

This style is for long hair and is called a rope braid. It is easy to do, although you may need a friend to help you! The important bit is to try and keep a tight hold of all three sections at the same time. If you don't keep hold of them, the braid may come undone when you tie it up at the end. This style takes a bit of practice, but looks really cool when it is finished!

1 Start by brushing your hair and tying it up with a band into a ponytail. You can do a high or low ponytail, you choose!

2 Split the ponytail into three sections and keep hold of them all. (This is where a friend can be handy!)

3 Take the right-hand section of hair. Twist it to the right a few times (clockwise) until it is in quite a tight twist.

4 Take the twisted section and pass it over the other two sections to the far left. Hold tight and try not to let it untwist.

5 Start again! Take the section on the right and repeat steps three and four. Keep going until your braid is long enough.

6 Finish the braid by tying it off with a band.

Sixer tip

Try this great style with your Six. Take it in turns so everyone gets her hair done!

Did you know?

- You have about 100,000 (that's a hundred thousand!) hairs on your head!
- **The world record for the longest hair is held by Xie Qiuping from China. Her hair is an amazing 5m 6ocm long!**
- If you lived in Ancient Egypt, you would probably have had no hair at all! Children's heads were often shaved to keep them cool and clean.

Brownie badges

Choosing which Brownie badge to do can be hard – there are just so many! Use this fun quiz to help you find the badges that are right for you!

Draw circles around the statements you agree with. Then count up how many of each colour you have circled. Look at the opposite page to see which badges you should try!

I hate sitting still!

I am good with technology.

I am always making things.

I want to be a sports star when I grow up.

I don't like being stuck indoors.

My dream is to be a pop star.

My best lessons are Maths and Science.

My favourite lesson is Art.

Seeing wild creatures is really exciting.

When I hear music, I have to dance!

I love putting on a show!

The Internet is great!

I love exploring new places.

I love feeling fit and healthy.

I'm going to be a fashion designer.

I'm always clowning around!

Camping is the best kind of holiday.

I love making up stories.

I like being the centre of attention.

I like learning new skills.

How many purple?

How many green?

How many pink?

How many orange?

How many blue?

Mostly purple...

You are an active type who is happiest on the move! Use your energy on some of these sporty badges.

- Agility
- Swimmer
- Watersports
- Sports
- Cyclist
- Rider
- Dancer
- Healthy heart

Mostly green...

You love the great outdoors, and everything that Nature has to offer. These badges will suit you down to the ground!

- Finding your way
- Out and about
- Brownie camper
- Gardener
- Widlife explorer

Mostly blue...

Practical and curious, you love getting to grips with the skills of modern life! Stay on the cutting edge with these badges.

- Communicator
- Computer
- First aid
- Science investigator
- Number fun

Mostly pink...

Artist, writer, craft person – you are truly creative. Express yourself with some of these badges.

- Writer
- Craft
- Designer
- Artist
- Toymaker

Mostly orange...

You were born to be a star! These badges will let you show off your performing skills!

- Musician
- Speaker
- Entertainer
- Circus performer

Going green

Make a recycled sign to give your family some great green tips!

Environment
Badge link

1 Cut one of the large sides off the cereal box. Turn it so the plain brown side is up.

You will need
- old cereal box
- scissors
- old magazines
- glue stick
- pens

2 Look through your magazines and find some really colourful pages. Cut out lots of small squares of bright colour, about 2cm by 2cm. It doesn't matter if they are not all exactly the same size!

3 Stick your coloured squares around the edges of the cardboard, to make a funky mosaic border.

4 Now write your green tips in the middle of the sign. Here are some ideas:
- Turn off dripping taps!
- Keep the fridge door closed!
- Remember to recycle!
- Don't waste water!

See if you can think of any more!

5 When you have finished, stick your sign up in the kitchen. It will help your family to go green and look after the planet!

Mmm-muffins!

There's a double dose of chocolate in these yummy muffins!

Ingredients

- 150g self-raising flour
- 1 tablespoon cocoa powder
- ½ teaspoon baking powder
- 50g sugar
- 1 egg
- 50ml cooking oil
- 100ml milk
- 100g chocolate chips

Badge link

Cook

Cook

You will need

- sieve
- bowl
- mug
- fork
- wooden spoon
- muffin cases
- baking tray
- oven gloves
- wire cooling tray

1 Sift the flour, cocoa powder and baking powder into a bowl. Stir in the sugar.

2 Break the egg into a mug and beat it lightly with a fork. Add it to the bowl. Add the oil, milk and chocolate chips. Stir the mixture a few times until it is just mixed. It is very important not to stir muffins too much, or they will be heavy.

3 Spoon the mixture into your muffin cases and stand them on a baking tray. Bake them at 200°C/400°F/gas mark 6 for 20 minutes. When they are done, carefully take them out of the oven and put them on a wire tray to cool. (Or you could eat them warm!)

Be safe

Illustrated by Cathi Mingus

71

It's good to

Can you speak another language? Try and learn some of these words – then you can make friends all over the world!

Welsh

Hello / good morning	Helo / bore da (hello / borr-e dah)
My name is...	Fy enw ydyw... (vy en-yoo oo-doo)
Please	Os gwelwch yn dda (oys gwel-ah un thar)
Thank you	Diolch (dee-olh)
Goodbye	Hwyl fawr (hoy-el vowr)
1	Un (een)
2	Dau (dy)
3	Tri (tree)
4	Pedwar (ped-wah)
5	Pump (pimp)

Spanish

Hello	Hola (oh-la)
My name is...	Me llamo... (me lee-ya-mo)
Please	Por favor (poor fa-voor)
Thank you	Gracias (gra-see-ass)
Goodbye	Adios (add-ee-oss)
1	Uno (oo-no)
2	Dos (doss)
3	Tres (trez)
4	Cuatro (kwa-tro)
5	Cinco (sin-co)

Yoruba

Hello	Bawoni (ba-wo-ni)
My name is...	Oruko mi ni.... (o-roo-ko mee-ne)
Please	Jowo (ja-wo)
Thank you	Oshe (o-shay)
Goodbye	Odabo (o-da-bo)
1	Ookan (oo-con)
2	Eeji (ay-jee)
3	Eeta (ay-ta)
4	Eerin (air-in)
5	Aarun (a-run)

talk!

Communicator

World traveller

World issues

Polish

Hello	Cześć (chesh-ch)
My name is...	Moje imę jest... (mo-yay y-mee-en yest)
Please	Proszę (pross-shen)
Thank you	Dziękuję (djin-koo-yen)
Goodbye	Do widzenia (doh vee-zen-ya)

1 Jeden (yay-den)
2 Dwa (dva)
3 Trzy (tshee)
4 Cztery (ch-tery)
5 Pięć (pee-ench)

Japanese

Hello	Ohio / konnichiwa (o-hi-oh / kon-ee-chee-wa)
My name is...	Watashi wa... desu (wa-tash-ee-wa... dess-oo)
Please	Kudasai (koo-dass-eye)
Thank you	Arigato (ar-i-gat-o)
Goodbye	Sayonara (sigh-oh-nar-a)

1 Ichi (itchy)
2 Ni (nee)
3 San (san)
4 Shi (shee)
5 Go (go)

Hindi

Hello	Namaste (na-mass-tay)
My name is...	Mera naam... hai (may-ra naam... hey)
Please	Kripya (krip-ya)
Thank you	Dhanyavaad / shukriya (dan-ya-vaad / shook-ree-ya)
Goodbye	Phir milenge (fearr mi-len-gay)

1 Ek (ake)
2 Do (doh)
3 Teen (teen)
4 Chaar (char)
5 Paanch (paanch)

Fly away

Make and fly this brilliant kite!

1 First, make the kite frame. Take the two canes and make a cross with them. Tie the sticks tightly together, making sure the cross stays at right angles.

You will need

- two pieces of garden cane, one 60cm and one 45cm long
- ball of plastic garden string or fishing line
- scissors
- sticky tape
- large carrier bag or bin liner

2 Ask an adult to cut notches in the ends of the canes, so that you can wrap the string around them. Do not try to do this bit yourself.

3 Take the ball of string and tie the end to the centre of your frame. Loop the string twice around the cross through the notches. Start at the top of the frame and keep the string tight. Bring the string back to the centre and tie it firmly. Trim the ends and stick them down neatly with tape.

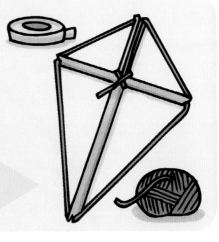

4 Cut a piece of string 75cm long. Tie one end to the top of the kite and the other end to the bottom. Stick tape over the knots to hold them in place. This string is called the bridle. Cut another piece of string about 130cm long and tie it to the bottom of the kite. This will make the tail.

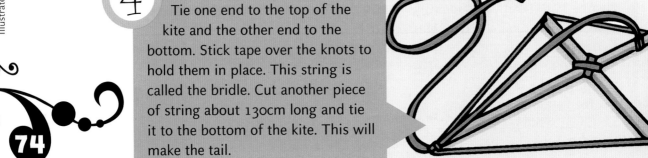

Illustrated by Stuart Lynch

5 Cut open your carrier bag or bin liner. Place the frame on the plastic. Cut around the frame, leaving edges at least 2cm wide all the way round.

6 Fold the edges over the frame and tape them down. Fold the corners down neatly and stick them in place.

7 Now make the bows for the kite's tail. Cut out ten squares from the leftover scraps of carrier bag. Each square should be about 10 x 10cm. Bunch each one into a bow shape and tie them along the tail, about 10cm apart.

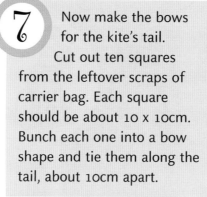

Craft
GLUE

Badge link

8 Finally, take the ball of string and tie the end to the bridle, about a third of the way down. This is your flying string and you're now ready to fly! Make sure you fly your kite only in open spaces with no power lines or trees around.

Answers

Did you solve all the puzzles?

Puzzle 1

Sandy is exactly the same as Honey.

Puzzle 2

The last direction is **North**.

Mind-benders (pages 10-11)

Puzzle 3

The creatures are: lizard, crocodile, snake, tortoise, dragon, alligator. **Dragon** is the odd one out - all the others are real animals!

FINISH

START

Puzzle 4

The nine-letter word is **mountains**.

Puzzle 5

The letters spell **water**.

Puzzle 6

The hidden word is **jungle**.

start

finish

J	E	S	S	I	E
U	R	S	U	L	A
N	I	C	O	L	A
G	R	A	C	I	E
L	O	U	I	S	E
E	M	I	L	I	E

Fresh fruit (pages 16-17)

1 = Pomegranate
2 = Mango
3 = Passion fruit

4 = Lychee
5 = Kiwi fruit
6 = Watermelon

More mind-benders (pages 26-27)

Puzzle 7

The birds that appear in the worm are: robin, wren, sparrow, blue tit, vulture, crow, magpie. You would probably not see a **vulture** in a back garden!

Puzzle 8

Croc gets the burger.

Puzzle 9

Rock is not in the grid.

Puzzle 10

The hidden picture is a **tree**.

Treasure hunt! (pages 52-53)

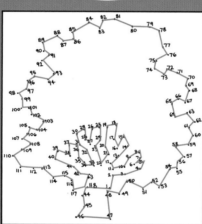

Puzzle 11

The pony's name is **Misty**.

Wonderful wildlife (pages 44-45)

1. a - red deer
2. b - beech
3. a - frogs, toads and newts
4. b - blue tit
5. b - slugs and worms
6. a - red admiral
7. c - foxglove
8. b - on a cliff
9. c - kits
10. b - greenfly